I0824238

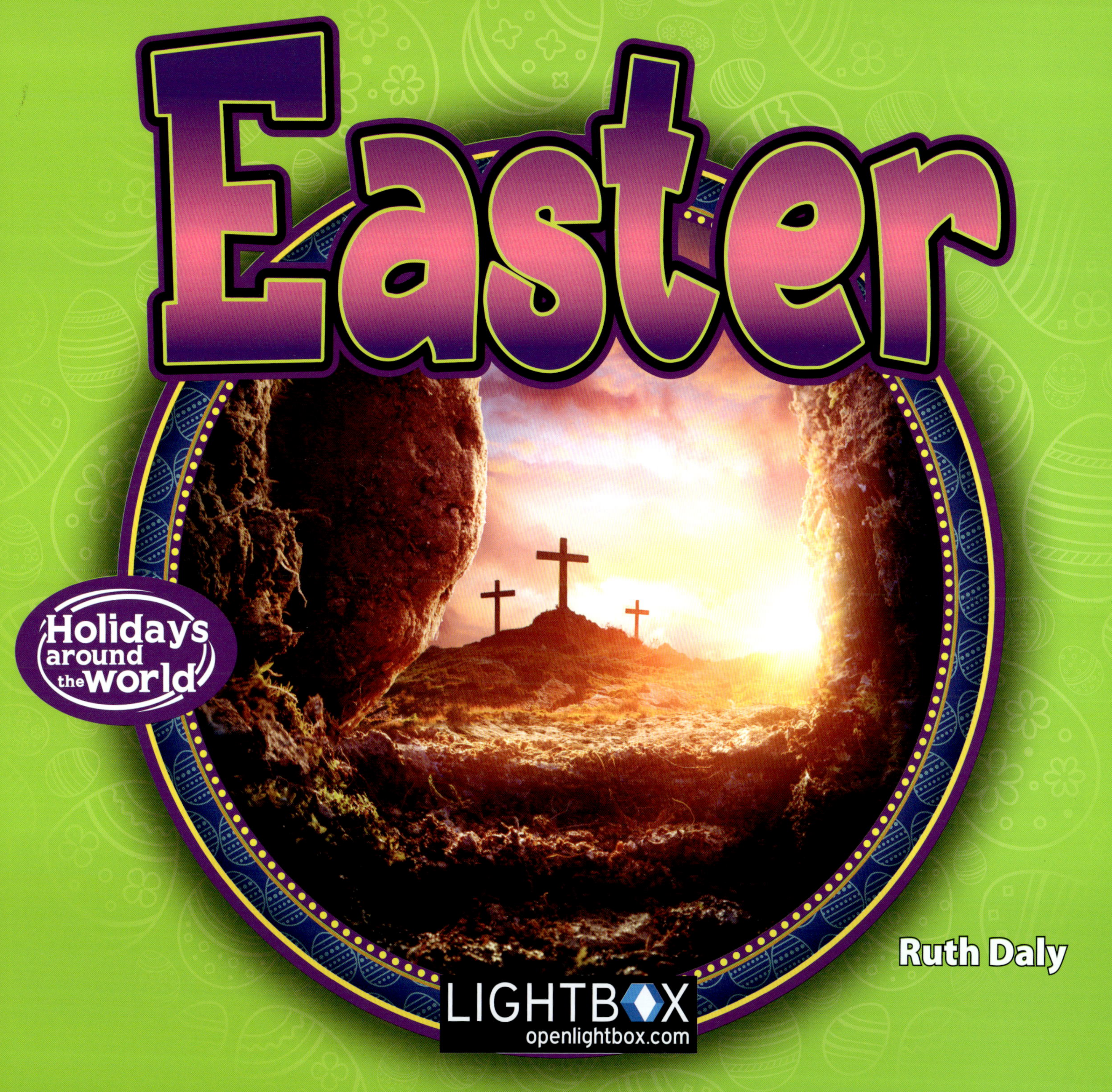
Easter
Holidays around the world
Ruth Daly
LIGHTBOX
openlightbox.com

LIGHTBOX

Go to **www.openlightbox.com** and enter this book's unique code.

ACCESS CODE

LBXW5589

Lightbox is an all-inclusive digital solution for the teaching and learning of curriculum topics in an original, groundbreaking way. Lightbox is based on National Curriculum Standards.

OPTIMIZED FOR

- ✓ **TABLETS**
- ✓ **WHITEBOARDS**
- ✓ **COMPUTERS**
- ✓ **AND MUCH MORE!**

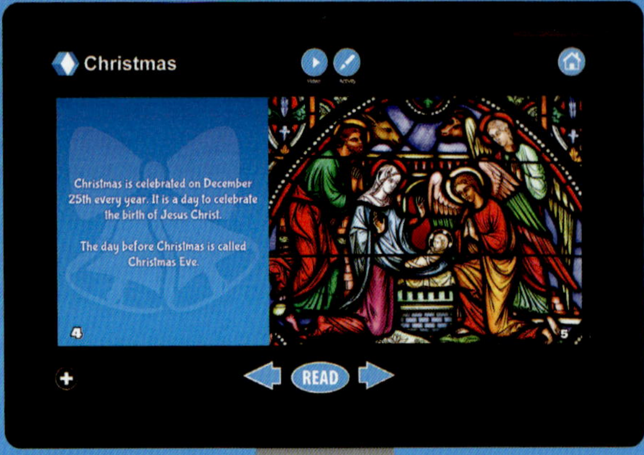

STANDARD FEATURES OF LIGHTBOX

 **AUDIO** High-quality narration using text-to-speech system

 **VIDEOS** Embedded high-definition video clips

 **ACTIVITIES** Printable PDFs that can be emailed and graded

 **WEBLINKS** Curated links to external, child-safe resources

 **SLIDESHOWS** Pictorial overviews of key concepts

 **INTERACTIVE MAPS** Interactive maps and aerial satellite imagery

 **QUIZZES** Ten multiple choice questions that are automatically graded and emailed for teacher assessment

KEY WORDS Matching key concepts to their definitions

VIDEOS

WEBLINKS

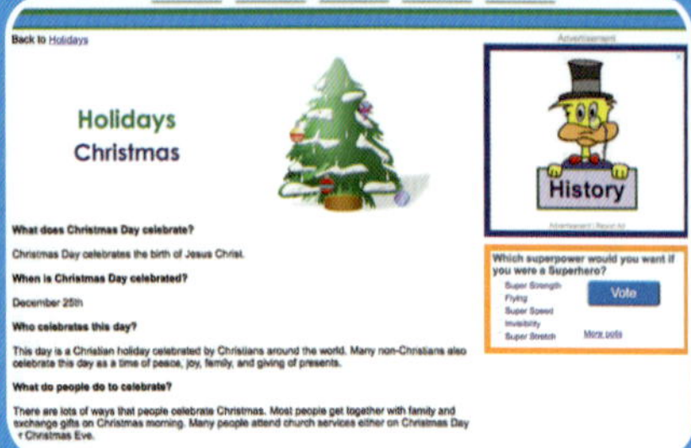

SLIDESHOWS

QUIZZES

Easter

CONTENTS

Easter is celebrated in March or April every year. It is a time when Christians remember that Jesus Christ died and came back to life.

Easter is always on a Sunday.

INRI
5

6

Easter is the most important holiday in the Christian faith. Christians believe that Jesus was the son of God.

The Easter Bunny brings chocolate, gifts, and candy on Easter. These treats are left in baskets.

10

Churches have special services at Easter. People pray and sing songs. They also light candles.

The Pope celebrates Easter with a service called Mass. This takes place in St. Peter's Basilica in Vatican City.

Groups of people go on Easter egg hunts. Children look for candy and chocolate eggs.

Hot cross buns are eaten at Easter. They are made with sweet bread and raisins. Each bun has the shape of a cross on top.

People go to Easter Parades. They may wear fancy hats called Easter bonnets.

The largest Easter Parade in the United States is in New York City.

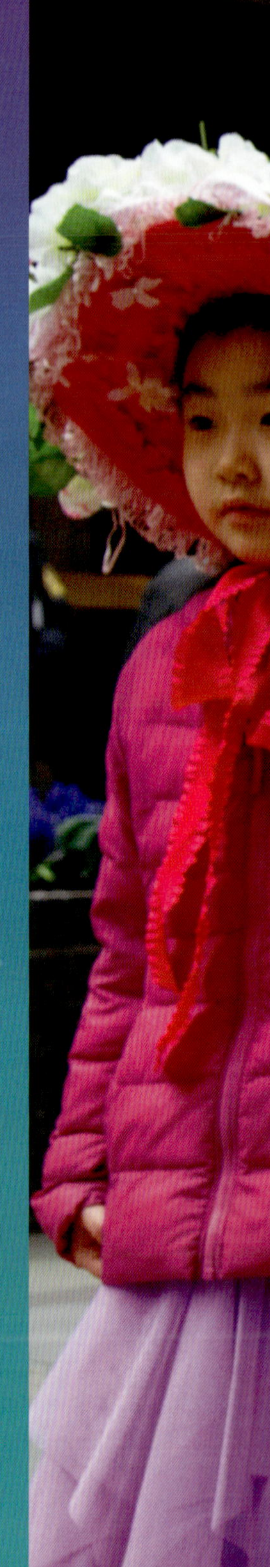

Lent is the 40 days before Easter. People give up treats or bad habits during Lent.

They also donate money and pray for people in need.

Painting eggs is an Easter tradition. The eggs are decorated with colors and patterns.

People also give each other candy, such as chocolate bunnies or jelly beans.

EASTER FACTS

These pages provide more detail about the interesting facts found in the book. They are intended to be used by adults as a learning support to help young readers round out their knowledge of each holiday featured in the *Holidays around the World* series.

Pages 4–5

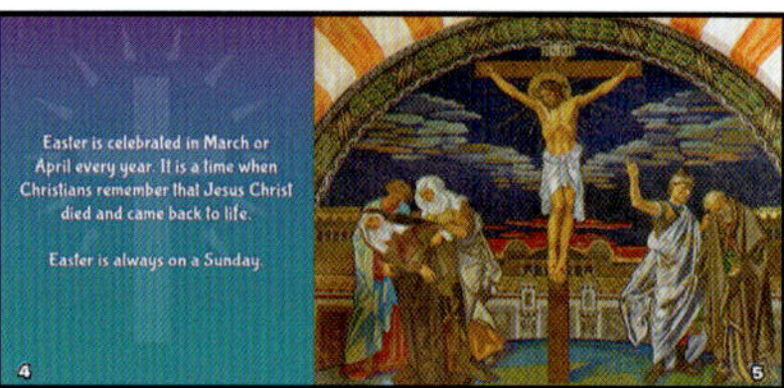

Easter is celebrated in March or April every year. The actual date of Easter changes from year to year, but it is always the Sunday after the first full moon of the vernal equinox, between March 22 and April 25. Orthodox Christians use a different calendar and celebrate Easter a few weeks later. The week before Easter is known as Holy Week. It includes Palm Sunday and Good Friday.

Pages 6–7

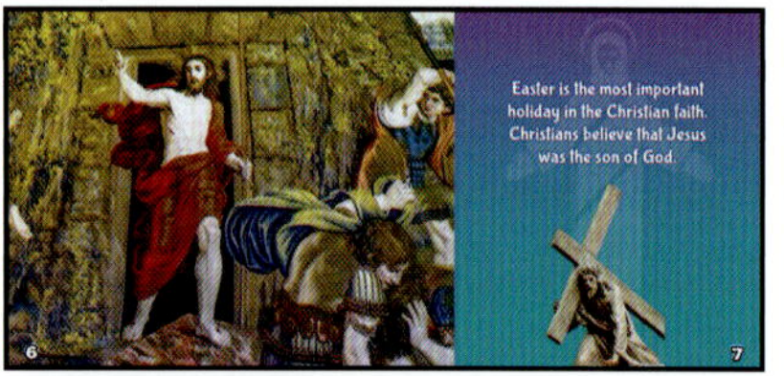

Easter is the most important holiday in the Christian faith. It is also the oldest Christian holiday. Good Friday is when Christians remember that Jesus Christ was crucified on a cross. They believe he died for the sins of the world, and that when Jesus rose from the dead three days later, it proved he was the son of God. They also believe his resurrection means their sins are forgiven and they can have eternal life after death.

Pages 8–9

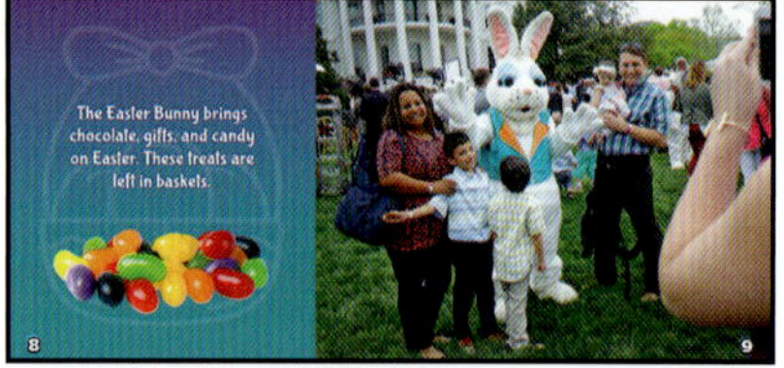

The Easter Bunny brings chocolate, gifts, and candy on Easter. The tradition of the Easter Bunny began in Germany, and European settlers brought the tradition to the United States in the 1700s. At that time, it was a hare known as the Osterhase, and children made nests in which it could lay its eggs. Over time, the Osterhase evolved into a bunny, and the nests became baskets.

Pages 10–11

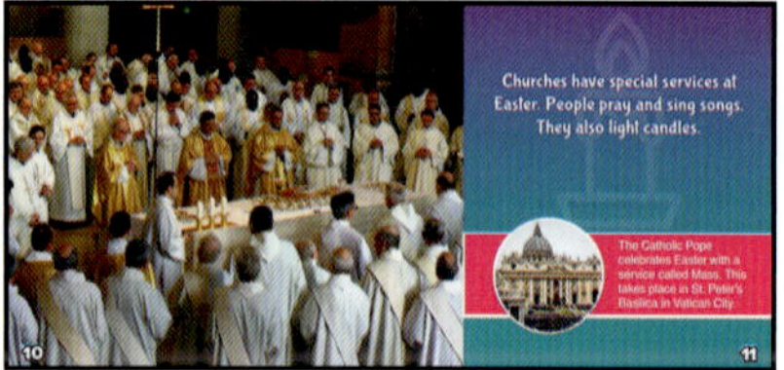

Churches have special services at Easter. Churches are often decorated with symbols that remind them of the Easter story in the Bible. This usually includes a purple cloth, because purple is a royal color, and Christians believe Jesus is a king. On Easter Day, churches have beautiful flower arrangements. Lilies are often used because they are a symbol of hope, new life, and springtime.

Pages 12–13

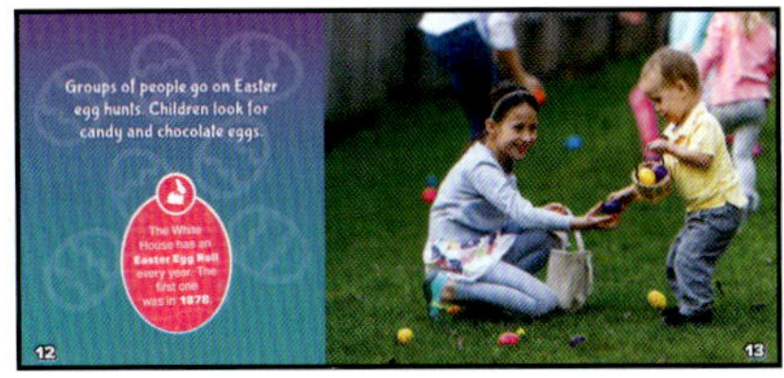

Groups of people go on Easter egg hunts. Real or chocolate eggs are hidden for children to find. Another popular activity is the Easter egg roll. An Easter egg roll is when children roll hard-boiled eggs down a hill. The winner is the child whose egg gets to the bottom first.

Pages 14–15

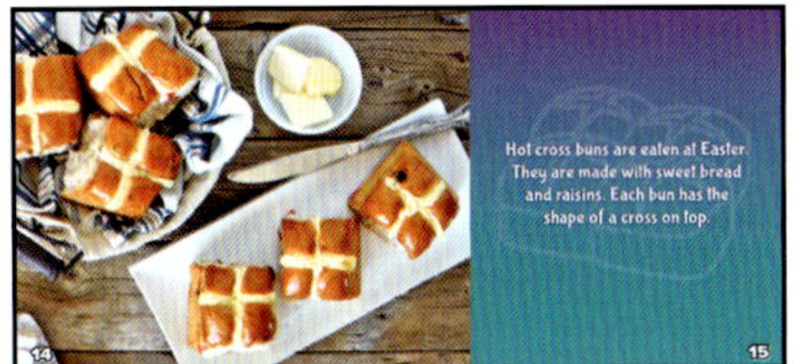

Hot cross buns are eaten at Easter. Many people celebrate with a huge meal on Easter Sunday, usually with roast lamb or baked ham as the main course. Ukrainian Christians bake a sweet bread called paska. This is decorated with religious symbols shaped from the dough and is taken to church in a basket on Easter.

Pages 16–17

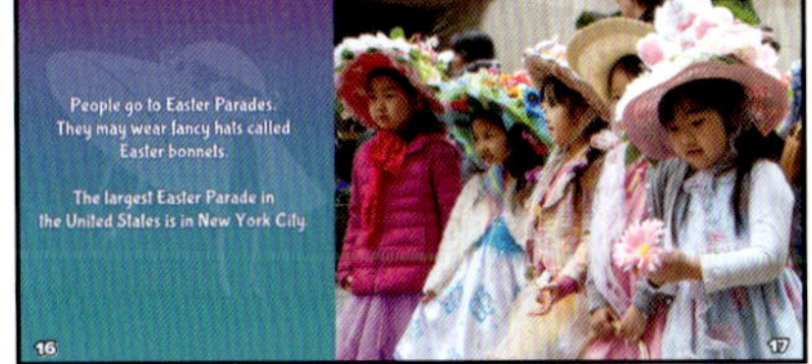

People go to Easter Parades. Easter Parades include decorated vehicles, marching bands, and people wearing costumes, including that of the Easter Bunny. In some places around the world, people watch the Easter story from the Bible performed by actors. This is called a Passion Play, named after Jesus's suffering.

Pages 18–19

Lent is the 40 days before Easter. It begins on Ash Wednesday. During this time, Christians spend time reflecting on spiritual matters. It is common for people to give up a bad habit, such as smoking or eating unhealthy food. They might donate money to charities that help homeless people or food banks. They also pray for people suffering injustice and hardship.

Pages 20–21

Painting eggs is an Easter tradition. Thousands of years ago, eggs were used by many ancient civilizations as a symbol of new life. The tradition of giving eggs at Easter is based on this. Jelly beans have been eaten at Easter since about 1930. Their popularity in the United States means that more than 16 billion are made just for this holiday alone.

KEY WORDS

Research has shown that as much as 65 percent of all written material published in English is made up of 300 words. These 300 words cannot be taught using pictures or learned by sounding them out. They must be recognized by sight. This book contains 62 common sight words to help young readers improve their reading fluency and comprehension. This book also teaches young readers several important content words, such as proper nouns. These words are paired with pictures to aid in learning and improve understanding.

Page	Sight Words First Appearance
4	a, always, and, back, came, every, in, is, it, life, on, or, that, time, to, when, year
7	important, most, of, the, was
8	are, left, these
11	also, at, city, have, light, people, place, songs, takes, they, this, with
12	an, children, first, for, go, groups, has, house, look, one, white
15	each, made
16	may, new, states
19	before, days, give, need, up
20	about, as, other, such

Page	Content Words First Appearance
4	April, Christians, Easter, Jesus Christ, March, Sunday
7	faith, God, holiday, son
8	baskets, Easter Bunny, candy, chocolate, gifts, treats
11	candles, churches, Mass, Pope, St. Peter's Basilica, services, Vatican City
12	egg, egg roll, hunts, White House
15	cross, hot cross buns, raisins, shape, sweet bread, top
16	bonnets, hats, New York City, parades, United States
19	habits, Lent, money
20	colors, jelly beans, patterns, tradition

Published by Smartbook Media Inc.
350 5th Avenue, 59th Floor New York, NY 10118
Website: www.openlightbox.com

Library of Congress Cataloging-in-Publication Data

Names: Daly, Ruth, 1962- author.
Title: Easter / Ruth Daly.
Description: New York, NY : Smartbook Media Inc., 2020. | Series: Holidays around the world | Audience: Ages 5-7 | Audience: Grades K-1 |
Identifiers: LCCN 2020004801 (print) | LCCN 2020004802 (ebook) | ISBN 9781510553224 (library binding) | ISBN 9781510553231 | ISBN 9781510553248
Subjects: LCSH: Easter--Juvenile literature.
Classification: LCC GT4935 .D35 2020 (print) | LCC GT4935 (ebook) | DDC 394.2667--dc23

LC record available at https://lccn.loc.gov/2020004801
LC ebook record available at https://lccn.loc.gov/2020004802

032020
110819

Printed in Guangzhou, China
1 2 3 4 5 6 7 8 9 0 24 23 22 21 20

Project Coordinator: Priyanka Das
Art Director: Terry Paulhus

The publisher acknowledges Alamy, Getty Images, iStock, and Shutterstock as its primary image suppliers for this title.